# SUMMER MATH WORKBOOK

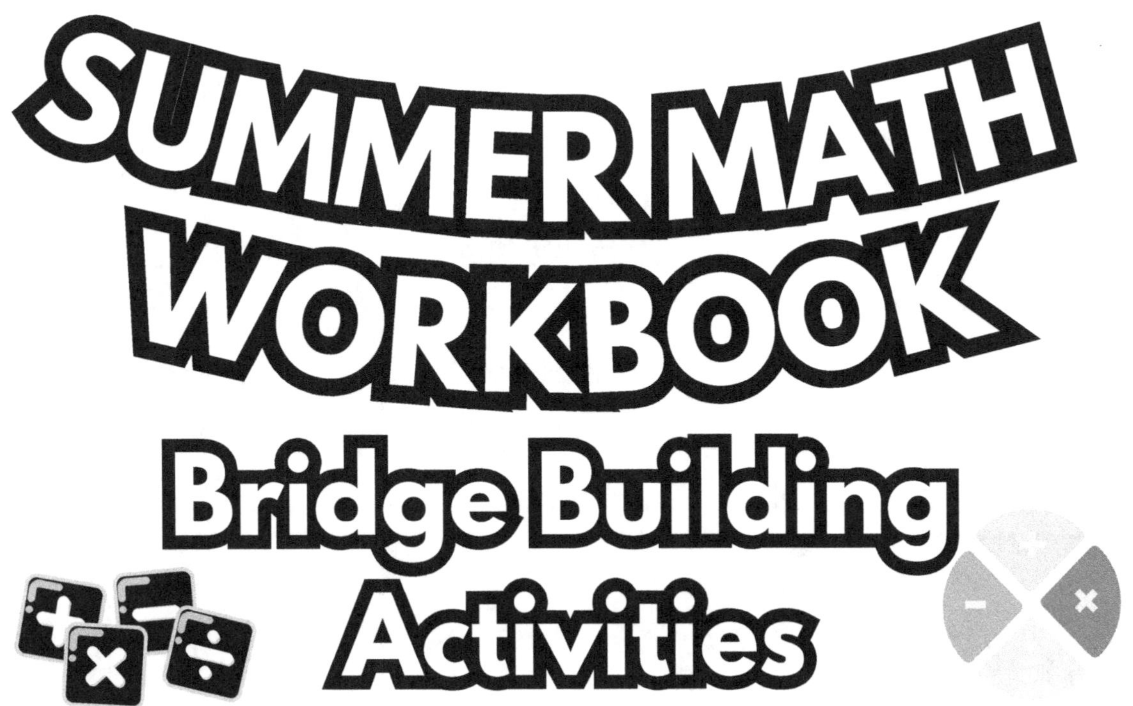

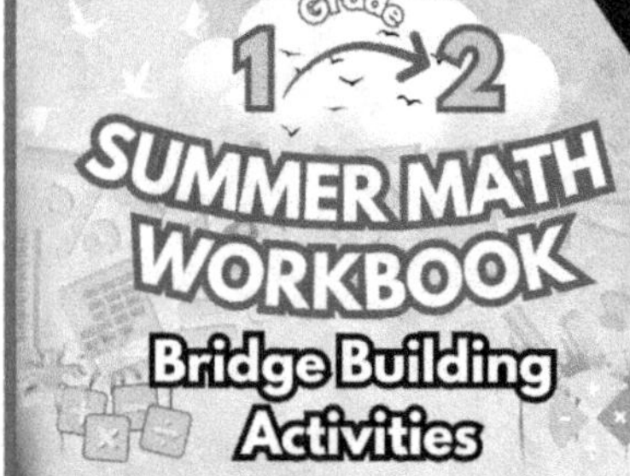


Grade
1 → 2
SUMMER MATH WORKBOOK
Bridge Building Activities
Number Sense
Addition and Subtraction
Place Value



Grade
2 → 3
SUMMER MATH WORKBOOK
Bridge Building Activities
Number Sense
Addition and Subtraction
Place Value



Grade
3 → 4
SUMMER MATH WORKBOOK
Bridge Building Activities
Number Sense
Addition and Subtraction
Place Value



Grade
4 → 5
SUMMER MATH WORKBOOK
Bridge Building Activities
Multiplication and Division
Place Value and Units
Fractions and Geometry



Grade
5 → 6
SUMMER MATH WORKBOOK
Bridge Building Activities
Multiplication and Division
Factors and Multiples
Fractions and Geometry



Grade
6 → 7
SUMMER MATH WORKBOOK
Bridge Building Activities
Arithmetic
Algebra
Geometry and Statistics



Grade
7 → 8
SUMMER MATH WORKBOOK
Bridge Building Activities
Ratio and Percentage
Algebra and Cartesian Plane
Geometry and Statistics



Grade
8 → 9
SUMMER MATH WORKBOOK
Bridge Building Activities
Ratio and Percentage
Algebra
Geometry and Graphing



Grade
9 → 10
SUMMER MATH WORKBOOK
Bridge Building Activities
Factoring and Distributing
Algebra
Geometry and Graphing

# Introduction

As parents and educators, we understand the pivotal role that mathematics plays in shaping a child's academic journey and future success. Yet, the path to mathematical proficiency can often seem daunting, filled with challenges and complexities. That's where the transformative power of Summer Bridge Building Activities books comes into play, illuminating the way forward with clarity, precision, and purpose.

Summer vacation is a time for rest and relaxation, but it also presents the risk of the "summer slide," where students lose some of the academic gains they made during the school year. Summer Bridge Building Activities books are specifically designed to tackle this challenge, ensuring that your child stays academically engaged and prepared for the upcoming school year. These books provide a seamless bridge from one grade to the next, reinforcing essential skills and introducing new concepts that will give your child a head start.

Imagine your child eagerly diving into the pages of a Summer Bridge Building Activities book, greeted by clear, engaging content that demystifies complex mathematical concepts. With each turn of the pages, they embark on a journey of discovery, encountering thoughtfully curated practice questions that reinforce learning and sharpen problem-solving skills. As they unveil the answers to those questions, a sense of accomplishment blossoms within them — a tangible reward for their hard work and dedication.

Summer Bridge Building Activities books transcend traditional educational tools; they are meticulously crafted to build a deep and enduring understanding of mathematics. These books follow a sequential and logical progression, starting from fundamental principles and advancing to sophisticated problem-solving strategies. Each chapter is designed to build on the previous one, ensuring a solid and comprehensive foundation for future learning.

Parents, we yearn for nothing more than to see our children thrive academically and personally. We want to witness the spark of inspiration ignited within them as they overcome academic challenges with confidence and poise. Summer Bridge Building Activities books serve as indispensable partners in this noble endeavor, offering not just practice questions but the keys to unlocking a world of academic and personal opportunities.

Visualize the pride on your child's face as they master a challenging math concept, the joy they experience when their efforts yield results, and the confidence they gain with each success. These pages are designed to make learning math a positive, enriching, and deeply rewarding experience that will benefit them throughout their academic journey and beyond.

For educators, Summer Bridge Building Activities books are invaluable allies in the quest to cultivate mathematical proficiency in the classroom. Accompanied by comprehensive guides and readily available answers, instructors can focus on mentoring and nurturing their students, secure in the knowledge that these books provide a robust framework for effective learning.

Within the pages of Summer Bridge Building Activities books lies not just the promise of academic excellence, but the seeds of a brighter future. By integrating these resources into your child's summer routine, you are bestowing upon them the gifts of confidence, curiosity, and a lifelong love of learning.

Invest in your child's future today with Summer Bridge Building Activities books — because every great journey begins with a single step, and this step can change everything. Keep the momentum of learning alive over the summer, and watch your child soar to new academic heights.

# Contents

Grade 7 - 9
PRE ALGEBRA WORKBOOK
BRIDGE BUILDING ACTIVITIES
Equations, Inequalities and Expressions
Linear Equations Graphing and Slope
System of Equations Quadratic Equations


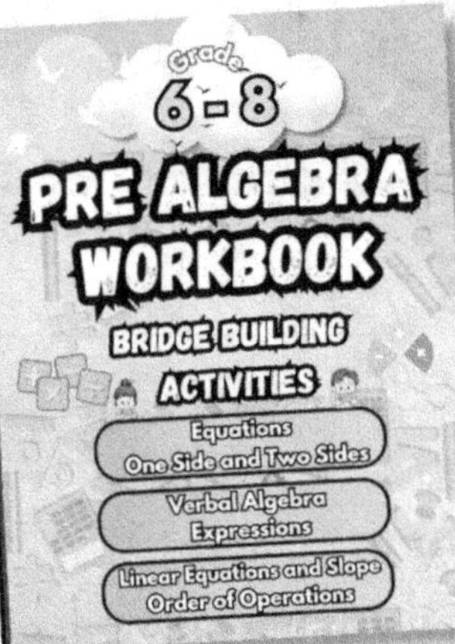

Grade 6 - 8
PRE ALGEBRA WORKBOOK
BRIDGE BUILDING ACTIVITIES
Equations One Side and Two Sides
Verbal Algebra Expressions
Linear Equations and Slope Order of Operations

Grade 5 - 6
PRE ALGEBRA WORKBOOK
BRIDGE BUILDING ACTIVITIES
Integers, Mixed Numbers Decimals and Fractions
Place Value Exponents and Roots
Percentage and Ratio Word Problems

PRE ALGEBRA WORKBOOK
for Beginners
Integers Fractions, Mixed Numbers
Place Value Exponents and Roots
Percentage Ratio Conversion

PRE ALGEBRA WORKBOOK
for Adults
Integers Percent and Ratio
Equations, Inequalities Expressions
Order of Operations


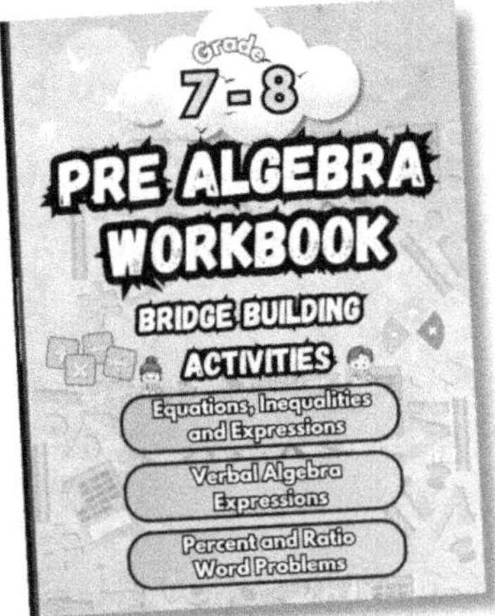

Grade 7 - 8
PRE ALGEBRA WORKBOOK
BRIDGE BUILDING ACTIVITIES
Equations, Inequalities and Expressions
Verbal Algebra Expressions
Percent and Ratio Word Problems

Grade 9 - 10
PRE ALGEBRA WORKBOOK
BRIDGE BUILDING ACTIVITIES
Equations and Inequalities Verbal Algebra
Linear and Quadratic Equations
System of Equations Polynomials


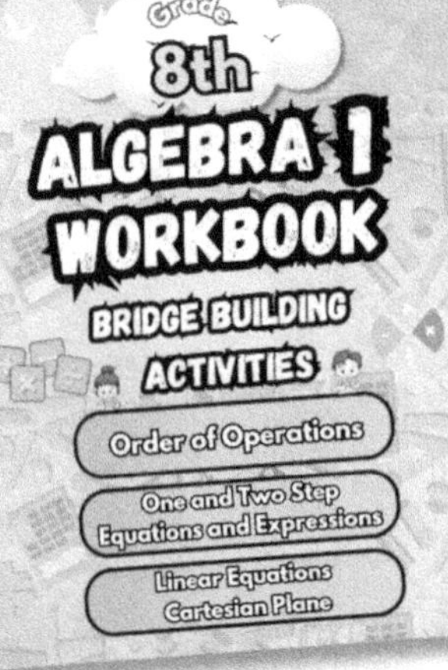

Grade 8th
ALGEBRA 1 WORKBOOK
BRIDGE BUILDING ACTIVITIES
Order of Operations
One and Two Step Equations and Expressions
Linear Equations Cartesian Plane

Grade 7 - 9
ALGEBRA 1 WORKBOOK
BRIDGE BUILDING ACTIVITIES
Integers Order of Operations
One and Multi Step Equations and Expressions
Linear, Quadratic Equations Equations One Side, Two Sides

## Operations with Integers

Positive and negative integers are whole numbers that can represent quantities greater than zero and less than zero, respectively.

**Positive Integers:** Positive integers are whole numbers greater than zero. They are denoted by the numbers 1,2,3,4...

**Negative Integers:** Negative integers are whole numbers less than zero. They are denoted by placing a negative sign ("-") before the numbers, such as $-1,-2,-3,-4,...$

The positive integers are used to represent the number of objects, scores, etc. whereas the negative integers can be used to represent debt, losses, temperatures below freezing points, etc.

**Let's solve some problems:**

### 1. 6 – ( – 8) – 9

- Start by simplifying within the parentheses:
$$- (-8) \text{ becomes } 8.$$
- Rewrite the expression with the simplified part:
$$6 + 8 - 9.$$
- Now perform addition and subtraction from left to right:
$$6 + 8 = 1\,4, \text{ then } 14 - 9 = 5$$

### 2. (– 5) – (– 3) + 10

$$(-5) + 3 + 10$$

$$(-5) + 3 = -2, \text{ then } -2 + 10 = 8$$

## Operations with Integers

Evaluate Expressions.

**1)** $3 - 10 - 9 =$

**2)** $(-5) - 4 =$

**3)** $(-1) - 6 + (-8) =$

**4)** $(-10) - 2 + (-4) =$

**5)** $7 - 5 + 7 =$

**6)** $5 - 7 - 5 =$

**7)** $(-4) - (-7) =$

**8)** $6 - (-10) =$

**9)** $8 + (-7) + 5 =$

**10)** $10 + (-8) =$

11) $7 - (-5) =$

12) $(-6) + (-7) + (-7) =$

13) $(-4) + (-3) - 5 =$

14) $(-5) - (-9) =$

15) $10 + (-1) =$

16) $8 + 6 - 2 =$

17) $(-7) + (-10) =$

18) $9 + (-8) - 10 =$

19) $8 - 5 - 6 =$

20) $10 + 10 - 3 =$

**21)** $(-9) + (-8) =$

**22)** $8 - 5 + 3 =$

**23)** $4 + 5 - 6 =$

**24)** $4 - 1 + (-2) =$

**25)** $(-3) + (-6) + 1 =$

**26)** $4 + 10 - 2 =$

**27)** $(-7) - (-8) =$

**28)** $(-5) - (-6) =$

**29)** $(-2) + (-4) - 4 =$

**30)** $8 + (-9) + 8 =$

**31)** $1 + (-1) + 2 =$

**32)** $(-10) - (-6) =$

**33)** $8 - (-4) =$

**34)** $6 + 6 - 8 =$

**35)** $1 - 6 + (-6) =$

**36)** $(-7) - (-2) =$

**37)** $(-2) - (-2) + 5 =$

**38)** $8 + 4 - 7 =$

**39)** $(-6) - (-8) + 4 =$

**40)** $(-9) - 3 =$

# Percentage

Percentage is a way of expressing a number as a fraction of 100. It is commonly used to represent proportions, rates, and comparisons. The symbol "%" is used to denote percentages.

To calculate a percentage, we multiply the given number by the appropriate fraction or decimal equivalent.

**How to calculate a percentage:**

**Convert Percentage to Decimal:** If the percentage is given as a percentage value (e.g., 25%), convert it to its decimal equivalent by dividing by 100.

$$\text{For example, 25\% as a decimal is } \frac{25}{100} = 0.25$$

**Multiply:** Multiply the decimal equivalent of the percentage by the given number. This gives us the portion of the number that represents the percentage.

$$100 \times 0.25 = 25\%$$

**Result:** The result is the calculated percentage value.

For example, to calculate 25% of 80:

Convert 25% to a decimal: 25% = 0.25.

Multiply 0.25 by 80: $0.25 \times 80 = 20$. The result is 20.

## Percentage

Find the percentage of given numbers.

1) 80% of ☐ = 320

2) 3% of 100 = ☐

3) 4% of 500 = ☐

4) 2% of ☐ = 12

5) 90% of ☐ = 810

6) 25% of 800 = ☐

7) 40% of ☐ = 360

8) 60% of ☐ = 540

9) 20% of ☐ = 4

10) 9% of ☐ = 45

11) [ ] of 500 = 35

12) [ ] of 200 = 12

13) 5% of [ ] = 45

14) 30% of [ ] = 120

15) [ ] of 700 = 105

16) 300% of [ ] = 1500

17) 50% of 400 = [ ]

18) [ ] of 200 = 150

19) [ ] of 600 = 60

20) [ ] of 300 = 24

**21)** [ ] of 300 = 3

**22)** 9% of 400 = [ ]

**23)** 35% of [ ] = 140

**24)** [ ] of 600 = 1200

**25)** [ ] of 600 = 30

**26)** 25% of 600 = [ ]

**27)** [ ] of 400 = 360

**28)** 3% of [ ] = 24

**29)** [ ] of 400 = 40

**30)** 75% of [ ] = 450

**31)** 300% of ☐ = 90

**32)** 60% of 100 = ☐

**33)** ☐ of 20 = 0.4

**34)** ☐ of 700 = 490

**35)** ☐ of 600 = 36

**36)** 4% of ☐ = 28

**37)** 20% of 400 = ☐

**38)** ☐ of 900 = 9

**39)** 8% of ☐ = 0.16

**40)** 7% of ☐ = 63

## Percent Word Problems

Percent word problems involve situations where percentages are used to calculate quantities or amounts. These problems often require converting percentages to decimals and then applying them to the given values.

**For example:**

Bella bought a pair of shoes for $90.00. If she paid an additional 90% for taxes, how much in total did she pay for the shoes?

- Bella bought a pair of shoes for $90.00.
- She paid an additional 90% for taxes.

Calculate 90% of $90:

Tax= 90% × 90

Tax= 0.90 × 90

Tax= $81

Add the tax amount to the original price:

Total cost= $90 + $81

Total cost= $171

## Percent Word Problems

**1)** If the number 50 is decreased by 44%, what is the value of the new number?

**2)** Emilia had a collection of 75 baseball cards. She gave away 76% of them. How many did she have left?

**3)** Kennedy bought a bag for $50.00. If she paid an additional 6% for sales tax, how much in total did she pay for the bag?

**4)** A store offers a 40% discount on all items. If Claire buys scrubs originally priced at $60.00, how much money did she save?

**5)** Aurora bought some forks for $50.00. If she paid an additional 44% for sales tax, how much in total did she pay for the forks?

**6)** Oliver bought a bicycle that cost $25.00 when it was new. If he eventually sold it for 76% of the original cost, how much was it sold for?

**7)** Adalyn bought a book for $50.00. If she paid an additional 92% for sales tax, how much in total did she pay for the book?

**8)** Carson earned $95.00 for a week's work. If he paid 40% of it in taxes how much did he pay in taxes?

**9)** In a survey of 50 people, 6% said they prefer cats over dogs. How many people prefer cats?

**10)** A school has 50 students. If 54% of them play football, how many students play football?

**11)** A store increases the prices of all items by 54%. If the bananas originally costs $50.00, what is the sale price?

**12)** A classroom has 50 students, of which 38% are girls. How many boys are in the classroom?

**13)** Noah's monthly sales of notebooks was $25.00. If he earned 76% of profit, what was his profit?

**14)** A car dealership sold 100 cars last month. If the sales increased by 92% this month, how many cars did they sell this month?

**15)** A restaurant makes a pizza that is 75 inches in diameter. If they want to increase the size of the pizza by 24%, what will be the new diameter?

**16)** A company wants to increase its revenue by 8%. If its current revenue is $75.00 million, what should be its new revenue?

**17)** A teacher gave a math test with 100 questions. If a student got 24% questions correct, how many questions were correct?

**18)** Molly bought a shoes for $15.00. If she paid an additional 40% for sales tax, how much in total did she pay for the shoes?

**19)** In a basket of 100 socks, 22% are red socks . How many are red socks?

## Ratio and Proportion Word Problems

We can use the concept of proportionality in solving many word problems, for example:

If a car travels 620 miles in six hours, how far can it travel in 12 hours?

Since the car travels a certain distance in a certain amount of time, we can assume that the distance traveled is directly proportional to the time taken.

Let $d$ be the distance the car can travel in 12 hours.

We can set up a proportion:

$$\frac{\text{Distance1}}{\text{Time1}} = \frac{\text{Distance2}}{\text{Time2}}$$

Substituting the given values:

$$\frac{620 \text{ miles}}{6 \text{ hours}} = \frac{d}{12 \text{ hours}}$$

Now, let's solve for $d$:

$$d = \frac{620 \times 12}{6} = \frac{7440}{6} = 1240$$

So, the car can travel 1240 miles in 12 hours.

**Ratio and Proportion Word Problems**

**1)** If a recipe calls for three eggs for every 10 cups of flour, how many eggs are needed for 19 cups of flour?

**2)** A zoo has a ratio of two monkeys to every seven lions. If there are 39 lions in the zoo, how many monkeys are there?

**3)** If eight workers can build a house in 18 hours, how many workers are needed to build the house in six hours?

**4)** If five workers can build a wall in 11 hours, how many workers are needed to build the wall in eight hours?

**5)** If a car travels 531 miles in seven hours, how far can it travel in 10 hours?

**6)** If a car travels 187 miles using 10 gallons of gas, how far can it travel using 17 gallons of gas?

**7)** If five painters can paint a house in 20 days, how many painters are needed to paint the same house in nine days?

**8)** Harper sells five computers for every eight purses. If there are 62 computers, how many purses are there?

**9)** A company has a ratio of three managers for every 30 employees. If the company has 116 employees, how many managers are there?

**10)** A charity received a donation of $1,047 from a company. If the donation was divided among five charities in the ratio 2:3:4:5:6, how much did the third charity receive?

**11)** A charity received a donation of $4,975 from a company. If the donation was divided among five charities in the ratio 2:3:4:5:6, how much did the fifth charity receive?

**12)** A car can travel 48 miles per gallon of gas. How many gallons of gas are needed to travel 103 miles?

**13)** If a recipe calls for three eggs for every eight cups of flour, how many eggs are needed for eight cups of flour?

**14)** If seven workers can complete a job in 16 days, how many workers are needed to complete the job in six days?

**15)** If a recipe calls for three teaspoon of salt for every four cups of flour, how much salt is needed for 20 cups of flour?

**16)** If a square has an area of 75 square meters, what is the length of each side of the square?

**17)** If eight chefs can bake 100 cakes in 17 hours, how many chefs are needed to bake the same number of cakes in five hours?

**18)** A car travels 146 miles in five hours. How far can it travel in six hours?

**19)** A recipe calls for three cups of sugar for every 10 cups of flour. If you have 15 cups of flour, how much sugar is needed?

**20)** If a map scale is 1 inch to eight miles, how far apart are two cities that are five inches apart on the map?

**21)** If a recipe calls for two cups of water for every five cups of rice, how much water is needed for seven cups of rice?

<u>**Order of Operations (PEMDAS)**</u>

The order of operations, often remembered by the acronym PEMDAS, stands for:

- **Parentheses**: Perform operations inside parentheses first.
- **Exponents**: Evaluate exponents (powers and roots) next.
- **Multiplication and Division**: Perform multiplication and division from left to right.
- **Addition and Subtraction:** Perform addition and subtraction from left to right.

The order of operations helps to clarify which operations should be performed first in a mathematical expression to ensure consistent and accurate results.

- **Parentheses**: Evaluate expressions within parentheses first. If there are nested parentheses, start with the innermost ones and work your way out.

  1. Example: $2 \times ( 3 + 4) = 2 \times 7 = 14$

- **Exponents**: Evaluate expressions with exponents (powers and roots) next.

  1. Example: $2^3 + 4 = 8 + 4 = 12$

- **Multiplication and Division**: Perform multiplication and division from left to right.

  1. Example: $2 \times 3 + 4 = 6 + 4 = 10$

  2. Example: $6 \div 2 \times 3 = 3 \times 3 = 9$

- **Addition and Subtraction**: Perform addition and subtraction from left to right.

  1. Example: $2 + 3 \times 4 = 2 + 12 = 14$

  2. Example: $10 - 4 \div 2 = 10 - 2 = 8$

## Order of Operations (PEMDAS)

Evaluate Expressions.

**1)** $(5 + 1) \times (8 + 8) =$

**2)** $(8 + 5) \div 6 =$

**3)** $3 \times 9 + 4 =$

**4)** $2 \times 7 + 10 =$

**5)** $(8 + 8)^2 + (3 + 4)^2 =$

**6)** $(3^2) \times (2^2) + 6 =$

**7)** $(7 + 7)^2 + (1 + 2)^2 =$

**8)** $(8 + 6) \div 1 =$

**9)** $8 \times 10 =$

**10)** $4 + 9 - 8 + 9 =$

**11)** $4 \times (8 + 3) =$

**12)** $(4 + 9)^2 + (7 + 2)^2 =$

**13)** $3 + 5 + 9 =$

**14)** $8 \times 4 =$

**15)** $5 \times (9 + 5) =$

**16)** $(3 + 5) \times (8 + 3) =$

**17)** $(8 \times 2) - (3 + 9) =$

**18)** $1(7 + 10) =$

**19)** $(2 + 4)(9 + 3) =$

**20)** $5 \times 6 \times 5 =$

**21)** $(9 + 6) \times (1 + 6) =$

**22)** $(9 + 5)(6 + 10) =$

**23)** $(4 + 3) \div 9 =$

**24)** $4(8 + 3) =$

**25)** $(8 + 6)(5 + 6) =$

**26)** $(7 + 6)(10 + 7) =$

**27)** $(1^2) \times (9^2) + 3 =$

**28)** $8 \times (10 + 5) =$

**29)** $(8 + 4)(2 + 4) =$

**30)** $(3 + 10)^2 =$

**31)** $(7 + 3)(5 + 8) =$

**32)** $(7 + 3)(8 + 9) =$

## Solving Equations (One Side)

Solving one-step equations involves performing a single operation to isolate the variable and find its value.

Let's solve an equation step by step: $16 + x = 31$

1. Identify the Goal:

   The goal is to isolate the variable $x$ on one side of the equation.

2. Simplify the Equation: Combine like terms on both sides of the equation, if necessary.

   The equation is already simplified.

3. Undo Addition or Subtraction: If there's addition or subtraction involving the variable, undo it by performing the opposite operation on both sides of the equation.

   Since $x$ is being added to 16, we'll undo this operation by subtracting 16 from both sides of the equation:
   $$16 + x - 16 = 31 - 16$$

4. Isolate the Variable: Ensure that the variable is alone on one side of the equation.

   $$x = 15$$

5. Check Your Solution: Substitute the value of $x$ back into the original equation to verify that it satisfies the equation.

   $$16 + 15 = 31$$

   $$31 = 31$$

The equation is balanced.

## Equations (One Side)

Solve for the variable.

**1)** $m - 1 = 0$

**2)** $y - 4 = 3$

**3)** $k \times 8 = 72$

**4)** $3 \times k = 18$

**5)** $6 \div m = 1$

**6)** $10 \div k = 10$

**7)** $9 + z = 16$

**8)** $8 + k = 18$

**9)** $y - 1 = 7$

**10)** $10 - y = 4$

**11)** $4 \times y = 20$

**12)** $6y - 3 = 27$

**13)** $10z + 7 = 77$

**14)** $x - 6 = 0$

**15)** $k + 10 = 17$

**16)** $5x - 5 = 0$

**17)** $6 \times m = 24$

**18)** $x + 4 = 14$

**19)** $3 \times z = 24$

**20)** $5 \times m = 40$

**21)** $x \times 9 = 9$

**22)** $x - 3 = 7$

**23)** $30 \div y = 5$

**24)** $10 \div k = 1$

**25)** $8 + 8x = 56$

**26)** $8 + x = 11$

**27)** $k + 10 = 16$

**28)** $y + 5 = 12$

29) $y - 8 = 1$

30) $m \div 2 = 3$

31) $6 \times k = 12$

32) $y \div 2 = 6$

33) $10 + x = 18$

34) $m \div 6 = 9$

35) $24 - 10x = 4$

36) $9x - 1 = 44$

37) $3x - 10 = 2$

38) $5x - 1 = 34$

## Equations (Two Sides)

A two-sided equation is an equation where both sides have expressions with variables and constants. The goal when solving a two-sided equation is to find the value of the variable that makes both sides equal.

For example: Let's solve an equation:

$$9 + 8x + 8 = 64 + x + 2$$

- Combine Like Terms: Simplify each side of the equation by combining like terms (terms with the same variable or constants).

$$9 + 8x + 8 = 64 + x + 2$$
$$17 + 8x = 66 + x$$

- Isolate the Variable: Use inverse operations to isolate the variable on one side of the equation.

subtract $x$ from both sides:
$$17 + 8x - x = 66 + x - x$$
$$17 + 7x = 66$$

subtracting 17 from both sides:
$$17 - 17 + 7x = 66 - 17$$
$$7x = 49$$

divide both sides by 7:
$$\frac{7x}{7} = \frac{49}{7} = x = 7$$

- Check Solution: Once you find the solution, substitute it back into the original equation to ensure it makes the equation true.

Substitute $x = 7$ back into the original equation:
$$9 + 8(7) + 8 = 64 + 7 + 2$$
$$9 + 56 + 8 = 64 + 7 + 2$$
$$73 = 73$$

## Equations (Two Sides)

Solve for the variable.

**1)** $6 + 6k = 94 - 5k$

**2)** $6x + 11 = 9x + 2$

**3)** $3 + 8z + 2 = 33 + z$

**4)** $145 - 8x = 9 + 9x$

**5)** $22 + z + \text{-}4 = 4 + 2z + 5$

**6)** $3x = 20 - x$

**7)** $9 + 5z + 1 = 44 - z + 8$

**8)** $43 - z + 11 = 1 + 6z + 4$

**9)** $5y + 1 = 9 - 3y$

**10)** $21 - y + 13 = 9 + 3y + 9$

**11)** $3z + 4 = 14 - 2z$

**12)** $6 + y = 2y$

**13)** $24 - k = 7k$

**14)** $66 - x = 6x + 3$

**15)** $7k = 6 + k$

**16)** $1 + 2m = 25 - m$

**17)** $2y = 12 - y$

**18)** $6 + y = 5y + 2$

19) $16 + x = 3x + 2$

20) $56 - z = 2 + 7z + 6$

21) $17 - k + 13 = 7 + 2k + 8$

22) $25 - x + 10 = 1 + 2x + 7$

23) $13 + z = 4 + 4z$

24) $16 + y = 4 + 8y + 5$

25) $3 + 4y + 7 = 15 - y + 5$

26) $8 + 2y + 9 = 22 - y + 16$

27) $5 + 8k = 29 - 4k$

28) $9 + 6k + 3 = 47 + k$

29) $2k = 8 + k$

30) $5x = 8 + x$

31) $33 + 6z = 9z + 6$

32) $161 - 8z = 8 + 9z$

33) $2x + 20 = 5 + 5x$

34) $2m + 7 = 15 + m$

35) $38 - 7x = 6 + 9x$

36) $6 + 3z + 6 = 27 - z + 13$

37) $21 - k = 3k + 1$

38) $2m = 2 + m$

## <u>Evaluating Equations</u>

Evaluating expressions involves substituting given values for variables in an expression and then performing the indicated operations to find the result.

For example: Let's evaluate  $4x - 10$, when $x = 3$:

Step 1: Substitute the given value for the variable:

Replace every occurrence of x in the expression $4x - 10$ with the given value, which is 3:

$$= 4(3) - 10$$

## Step 2: Perform the operations:

Perform the indicated operations according to the order of operations (PEMDAS - Parentheses, Exponents, Multiplication and Division, Addition and Subtraction):

$$= 4 \times 3 - 10$$

Step 3: Simplify:

Calculate the result:

$$12 - 10 = 2$$

## Solving Equations

Evaluate each expression when: $x = 6$

**1)** $8x + 4 =$

**2)** $7 - x =$

**3)** $(9x + 3) + (7x - 6) =$

**4)** $8(2 + x) =$

**5)** $6 \div x =$

**6)** $1(2x - 2) + 7(3 + x) =$

**7)** $1(6 + x) =$

**8)** $2(4x - 3) + 2(5 + x) =$

**9)** $\dfrac{x}{2} + 1 =$

**10)** $3(x) =$

## Solving Equations

Evaluate each expression when: $x = 1$

**1)** $1(10x - 4) + 4(1 + x) =$

**2)** $6(7x - 9) + 7(7 + x) =$

**3)** $1 + \dfrac{x}{1} =$

**4)** $10x + 3x - 7 =$

**5)** $6 \div x + 5 =$

**6)** $10x + 2x + 8x =$

**7)** $4 + \dfrac{x}{1} =$

**8)** $2x + 6 =$

**9)** $2x + 10 =$

**10)** $4x + 8x + x =$

## Solving Equations

Evaluate each expression when: $x = 7$

**1)** $7 \div x =$

**2)** $9 + (6x + 5) - 1 + (4x) =$

**3)** $9^1 + x^1 =$

**4)** $3x + 3 - 10x =$

**5)** $6x + 8 + (4x - 1) =$

**6)** $\dfrac{x}{7} + 3 =$

**7)** $6x + 6 - 9x =$

**8)** $x^1 + x - 10 =$

**9)** $5 + (9x + 9) =$

**10)** $2(7x - 9) + 7(1 + x) =$

## Solving Equations

Evaluate each expression when: x = 5

**1)** $10 + \dfrac{x}{5} =$

**2)** $3x + 4x - 10 =$

**3)** $x + 8 + 2x =$

**4)** $(x^1 + 5) - 10(5 + x) =$

**5)** $10x + 9 =$

**6)** $x - 3 =$

**7)** $5x + 6 =$

**8)** $x(10 + x) =$

**9)** $4x - 8 + 7x =$

**10)** $10x + 7 =$

## Solving Equations

Evaluate each expression when: $x = 2$

**1)** $2 \div x + 10 =$

**2)** $3 + \dfrac{x}{2} =$

**3)** $2 \div x =$

**4)** $10(1 - x) =$

**5)** $x + 3 =$

**6)** $5 + \dfrac{x}{1} =$

**7)** $4x + 10x - 5 =$

**8)** $10 + x =$

**9)** $3x + 5 =$

**10)** $10 \div x =$

## Solving Equations

Evaluate each expression when: $x = 6$

**1)** $1(4 - x) =$

**2)** $7x + 9 =$

**3)** $\dfrac{x}{3} + 9 =$

**4)** $5x^1 + 8x^1 =$

**5)** $7x - x =$

**6)** $9 + \dfrac{x}{2} =$

**7)** $7^1 + x^1 =$

**8)** $1 + (3x + 10) =$

**9)** $x - 6 =$

**10)** $7(2 - x) =$

## Solving Equations

Evaluate each expression when: $x = 7$

**1)** $(x^1 + 10) - 3(10 + x) =$

**2)** $5x - 6 =$

**3)** $3^1 + x^1 =$

**4)** $(x + 1) \div 1 =$

**5)** $2x + 7x - 8 =$

**6)** $4x + 7x - 8 =$

**7)** $6(9 + x) =$

**8)** $6x + 5 =$

**9)** $7x + 10x - 8 =$

**10)** $2x + 8 =$

## Solving Equations

Evaluate each expression when: $x = 4$

**1)** $x - 7 =$

**2)** $8x - 1 =$

**3)** $7 + (9x + 8) =$

**4)** $10 - x =$

**5)** $x + x =$

**6)** $3x + 3x + 9x =$

**7)** $7 - x =$

**8)** $6x + x + x =$

**9)** $2 + x =$

**10)** $(x^1 + 4) - 5(7 + x) =$

## Solving Equations

Evaluate each expression when: $x = 3$

**1)** $(9x + 2) + (7x - 1) =$

**2)** $x + 1 =$

**3)** $9x + 8 - 10x =$

**4)** $7x + 10 - x =$

**5)** $\dfrac{x}{1} + 7 =$

**6)** $9x - 6 =$

**7)** $8x + 8 - 9x =$

**8)** $(x + 5) \div 4 =$

**9)** $x - 2 =$

**10)** $7x + 10 =$

## Solving Inequalities

Inequalities are mathematical expressions that compare the relative sizes of two values. They are used to express relationships where one quantity is:

- "<" (less than),
- ">" (greater than),
- "<=" (less than or equal to),
- ">=" (greater than or equal to),
- and "≠" (not equal to) another quantity.

For example:

$$y + -10 \leq -8$$

To isolate $y$, we need to get rid of the constant term $-10$. Since $-10$ is being subtracted from $y$, we can undo this operation by adding 10 to both sides of the inequality:

$$y - 10 + 10 \leq -8 + 10$$

$$y \leq 2$$

To check the solution:

$$2 - 10 \leq -8$$

$$-8 = -8$$

The inequality is true when $y = 2$

## Solving Inequalities

1) $\dfrac{x}{-9} > -2$

2) $y - {-2} \leq 8$

3) $-24 \leq -12\,z$

4) $2 < -6 + x$

**5)**
$$8 < k + -5$$

**6)**
$$6 \geq k - -6$$

**7)**
$$-21y > 18$$

**8)**
$$\frac{x}{3} < -4$$

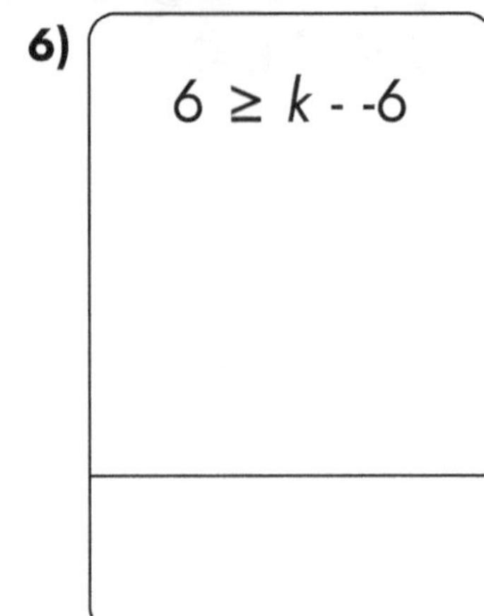

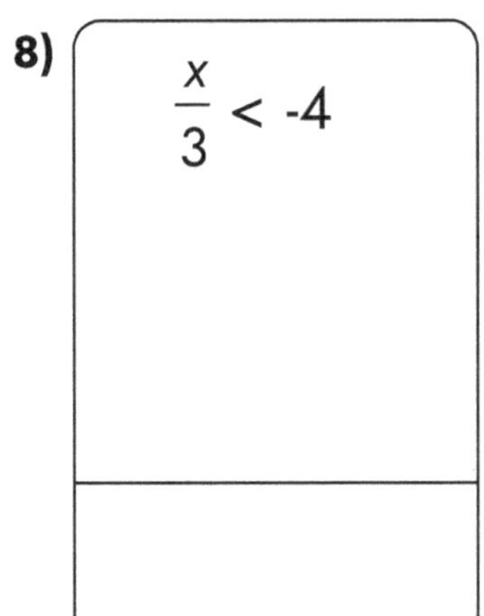

**9)**

$$-1 \leq x + -10$$

**10)**

$$\frac{m}{4} > 4$$

**11)**

$$7 \geq x - 6$$

**12)**

$$-12 \geq -20\,m$$

13)

$$m - 4 \leq 6$$

14)

$$-8 < 24\,y$$

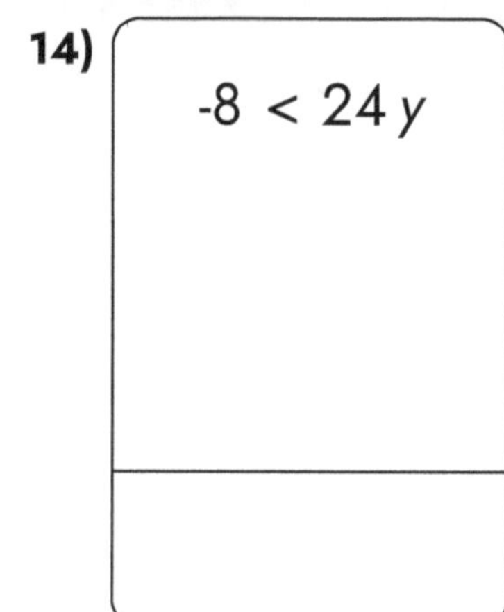

15)

$$-5 < -9 + k$$

16)

$$\frac{x}{-7} > 6$$

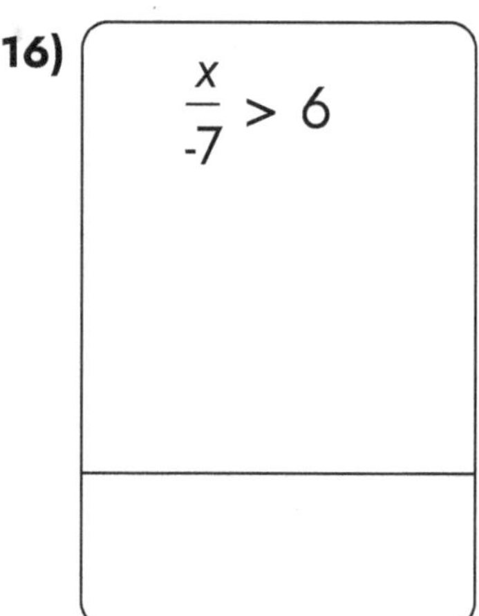

17)

$$\frac{x}{-6} \geq -1$$

18)

$$6z < -6$$

19)

$$z + 6 > -7$$

20)

$$6 \leq 5 - x$$

**21)** $-5 + y \geq 2$

**22)** $-7 - z > -1$

**23)** $6 \leq -6\,m$

**24)** $6 \geq \dfrac{m}{6}$

**25)**

$$\frac{k}{6} > -3$$

**26)**

$$8 < k - -1$$

**27)**

$$-4 \geq -5 + z$$

**28)**

$$-8\,m \leq 10$$

<u>**Simplifying Expressions**</u>

It involves combining like terms and performing operations to make the expression easier to understand and work with.

Let's simplify the expression:

$$2x - 2x + 8 + 4$$

- Combine like terms: First, we look for terms with the same variable and exponent. In this expression, $2x$ and $-2x$ are like terms, so they can be combined:

$$2x - 2x = 0$$

- Substitute the simplified terms: After combining the like terms, the expression becomes:

$$0 + 8 + 4$$

- Combine the remaining terms: Now, we add the constants together:

$$8 + 4 = 12$$

# Simplify Expressions

**1)** $-11 + 15y - 13y - 12 + 15y$

**2)** $-8 - z + 9 - 19z$

**3)** $4 + 6(-17m + 13)$

**4)** $z - 2z + 4z + 4 + 4$

**5)** $-14 - 20y + 16y - 19 + 20y$

**6)** $-14 + 11k - 4k - 17 - 7k$

**7)** $-8y + 18 + 14y$

**8)** $m - 11m$

9) $-13y - 14 - 3y$

10) $-2z + 1 - z$

11) $9x - 1 - 8x + 2 - 13$

12) $-18k + 17 + 16k$

13) $-7z + 13z + 15 - 15z$

14) $m + 3m$

15) $6z - 17z$

16) $19 + 12m - 20m$

**17)** $14y + 12 + 6y$

**18)** $-10y + 18 + 12y$

**19)** $-15 + 19z - 2z - 10 - 14z$

**20)** $3y + 10 - 20y - 8 + 2y - 7$

**21)** $-18y - y$

**22)** $18k + 4 - k + 17 + k + 5$

**23)** $2m + m$

**24)** $16x - 14 - 11x + 1$

## **Graphing Linear Equation**

Graphing a linear equation involves plotting the points that satisfy the equation on a coordinate plane and connecting them to form a straight line. Linear equations are equations of the form $y = mx + b$, where $m$ represents the slope of the line, and $b$ represents the y-intercept, the point where the line intersects the y-axis.

To graph a linear equation:

1. Identify the slope ($m$) and y-intercept ($b$) from the equation.

2. Plot the y-intercept $(0,b))$ as a point on the y-axis.

3. Use the slope to find additional points on the line. The slope represents the change in y for every unit change in x.

4. Connect the points to form a straight line.

For example, to graph the equation:

$$y = \frac{9}{4}x - 8$$

1. Identify the slope and y-intercept: The slope is $\frac{9}{4}$, and the y-intercept is −8.

2. Plot the y-intercept: Plot the point (0,−8).

3. Use the slope to plot additional points:  the slop is $\frac{9}{4}$ to find another point. we will move up 9 units and 4 units to the right from the y-intercept to find another point.

4. Draw the line: Once we have at least two points, we can draw a straight line.

We can continue this process to plot more points and extend the line further if needed.

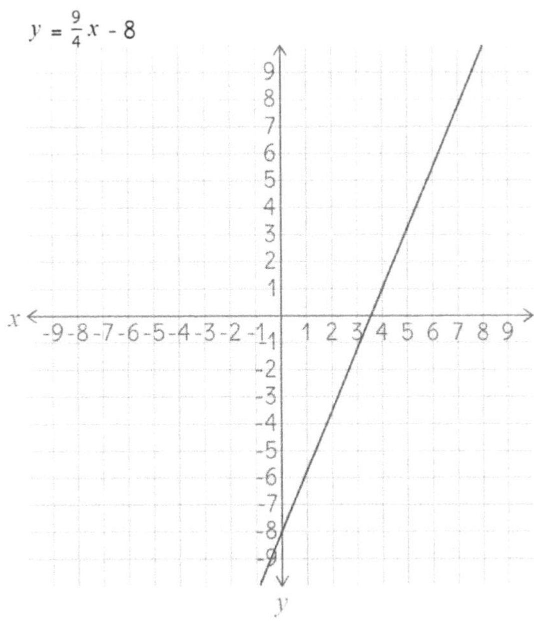

## Graphing Linear Equations

1) $y = -3x + 1$

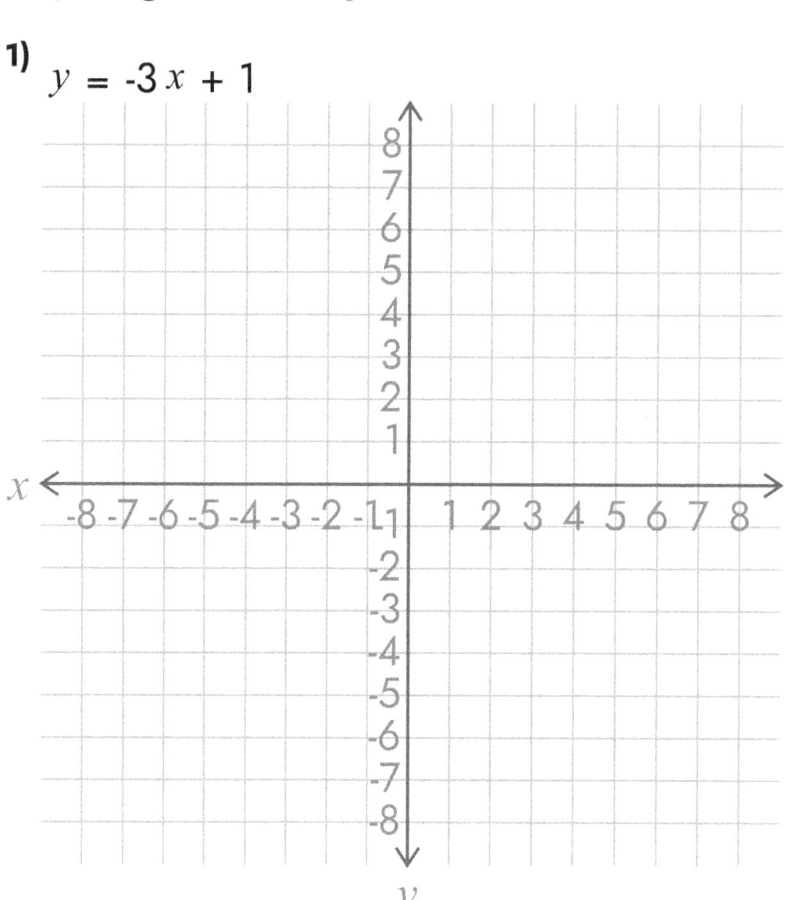

**2)** $y = \dfrac{1}{4}x + 5$

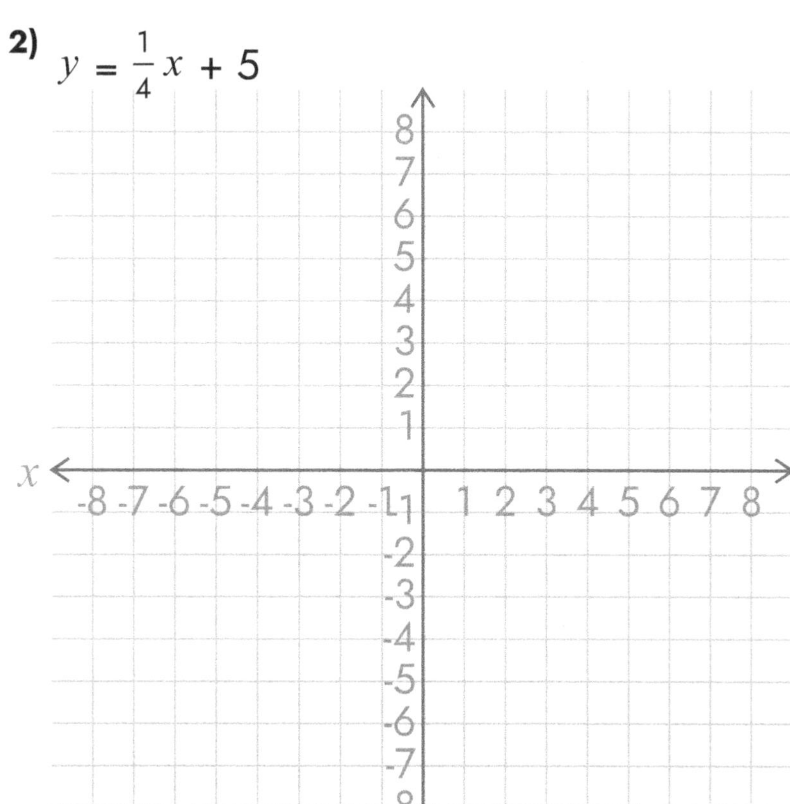

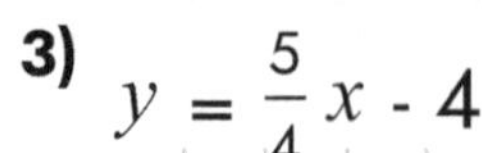


**3)** $y = \dfrac{5}{4}x - 4$

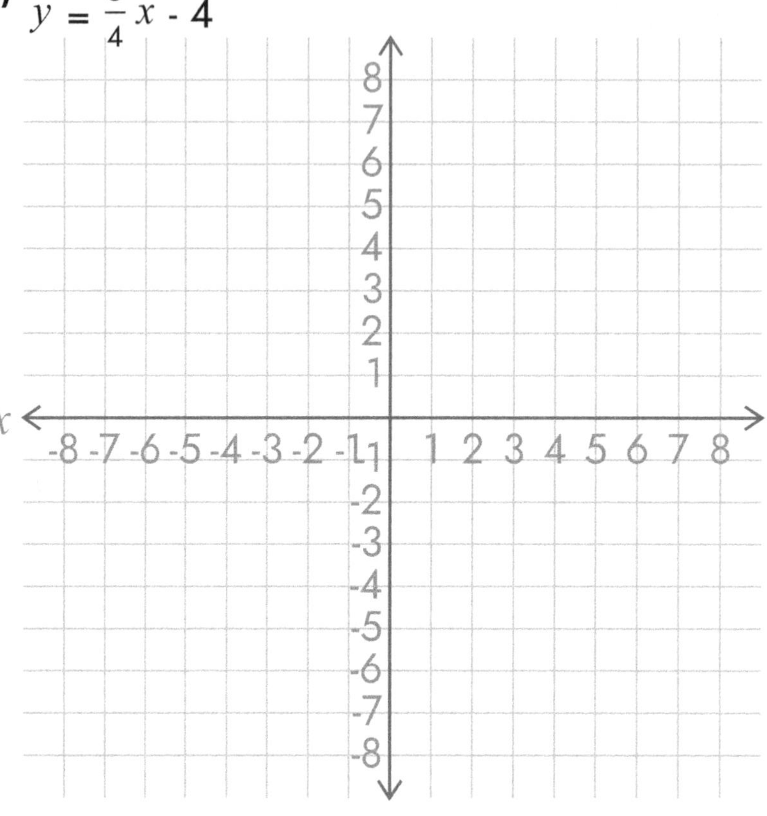

**4)** 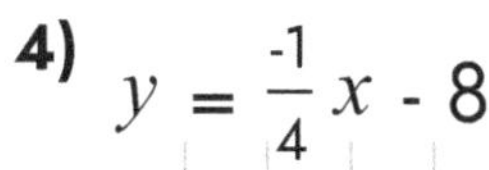

$$y = \frac{-1}{4}x - 8$$

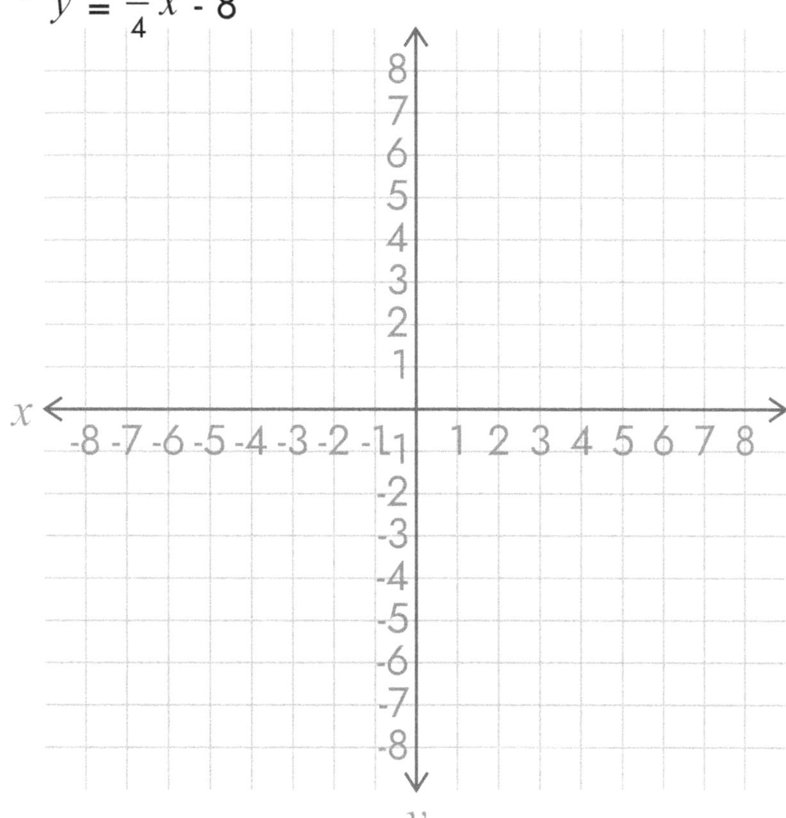

**5)** $y = \dfrac{3}{4}x - 6$

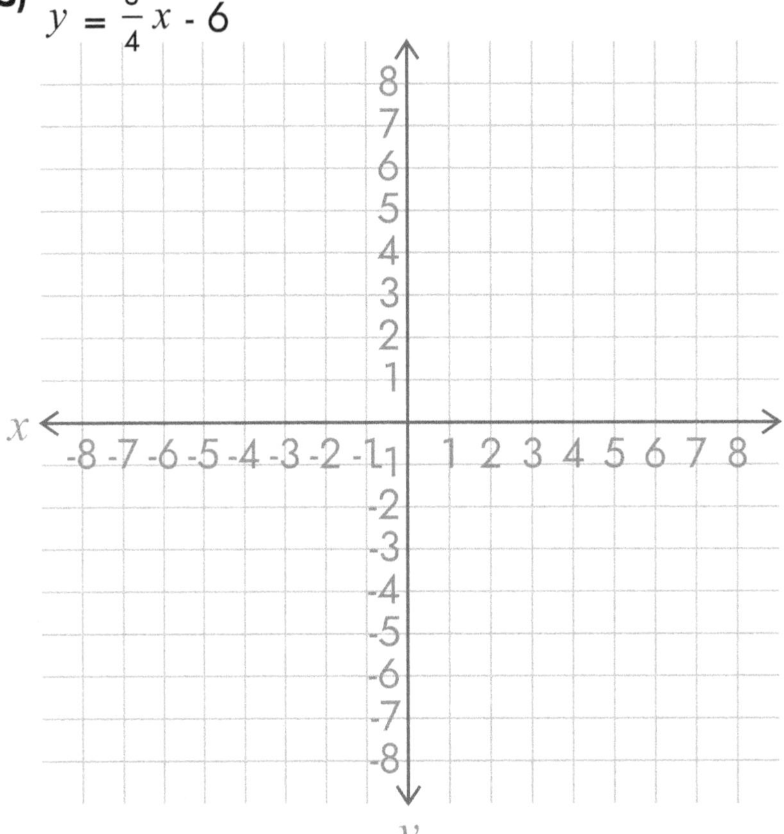

# ANSWERS

**Page 1: Operations with Integers**

**1.** -16 **2.** -9 **3.** -15 **4.** -16 **5.** 9 **6.** -7 **7.** 3 **8.** 16 **9.** 6

**10.** 2 **11.** 12 **12.** -20 **13.** -12 **14.** 4 **15.** 9 **16.** 12 **17.** -17 **18.** -9

**19.** -3 **20.** 17 **21.** -17 **22.** 6 **23.** 3 **24.** 1 **25.** -8 **26.** 12 **27.** 1

**28.** 1 **29.** -10 **30.** 7 **31.** 2 **32.** -4 **33.** 12 **34.** 4 **35.** -11 **36.** -5

**37.** 5 **38.** 5 **39.** 6 **40.** -12

**Page 5: Percentage**

**1.** 400 **2.** 3 **3.** 20 **4.** 600 **5.** 900 **6.** 200 **7.** 900

**8.** 900 **9.** 20 **10.** 500 **11.** 7% **12.** 6% **13.** 900 **14.** 400

**15.** 15% **16.** 500 **17.** 200 **18.** 75% **19.** 10% **20.** 8% **21.** 1%

**22.** 36 **23.** 400 **24.** 200% **25.** 5% **26.** 150 **27.** 90% **28.** 800

**29.** 10% **30.** 600 **31.** 30 **32.** 60 **33.** 2% **34.** 70% **35.** 6%

**36.** 700 **37.** 80 **38.** 1% **39.** 2 **40.** 900

**Page 9: Percent Word Problems**

**1.** 28 **2.** 18 **3.** $53.00 **4.** $24.00 **5.** $72.00 **6.** $19.00

**7.** $96.00 **8.** $38.00 **9.** 3 **10.** 27 **11.** $77.00 **12.** 31

**13.** $19.00 **14.** 192 **15.** 93 **16.** $81.00 **17.** 24 **18.** $21.00

**19.** 22

**Page 14: Ratio and Proportion Word Problems**

**1.** 5.7 **2.** 11.14 **3.** 24 **4.** 6.88 **5.** 758.57 **6.** 317.9

**7.** 11.11 **8.** 99.2 **9.** 11.6 **10.** 209.4 **11.** 1,492.5 **12.** 2.15

**13.** 3     **14.** 18.67     **15.** 15     **16.** 8.66     **17.** 27.2     **18.** 175.2

**19.** 4.5     **20.** 40     **21.** 2.8

## Page 21: Order of Operations (PEMDAS)

**1.** 96    **2.** 2.2    **3.** 31    **4.** 24    **5.** 305    **6.** 42    **7.** 205    **8.** 14

**9.** 80    **10.** 14    **11.** 44    **12.** 250    **13.** 17    **14.** 32    **15.** 70    **16.** 88

**17.** 4    **18.** 17    **19.** 72    **20.** 150    **21.** 105    **22.** 224    **23.** 0.8    **24.** 44

**25.** 154    **26.** 221    **27.** 84    **28.** 120    **29.** 72    **30.** 169    **31.** 130    **32.** 170

## Page 25: Equations (One Side)

**1.** $m = 1$    **2.** $y = 7$    **3.** $k = 9$    **4.** $k = 6$    **5.** $m = 6$    **6.** $k = 1$

**7.** $z = 7$    **8.** $k = 10$    **9.** $y = 8$    **10.** $y = 6$    **11.** $y = 5$    **12.** $y = 5$

**13.** $z = 7$    **14.** $x = 6$    **15.** $k = 7$    **16.** $x = 1$    **17.** $m = 4$    **18.** $x = 10$

**19.** $z = 8$    **20.** $m = 8$    **21.** $x = 1$    **22.** $x = 10$    **23.** $y = 6$    **24.** $k = 10$

**25.** $x = 6$    **26.** $x = 3$    **27.** $k = 6$    **28.** $y = 7$    **29.** $y = 9$    **30.** $m = 6$

**31.** $k = 2$    **32.** $y = 12$    **33.** $x = 8$    **34.** $m = 54$    **35.** $x = 2$    **36.** $x = 5$

**37.** $x = 4$    **38.** $x = 7$

## Page 29: Equations (Two Sides)

**1.** $k = 8$    **2.** $x = 3$    **3.** $z = 4$    **4.** $x = 8$    **5.** $z = 9$    **6.** $x = 5$    **7.** $z = 7$

**8.** $z = 7$    **9.** $y = 1$    **10.** $y = 4$    **11.** $z = 2$    **12.** $y = 6$    **13.** $k = 3$    **14.** $x = 9$

**15.** $k = 1$    **16.** $m = 8$    **17.** $y = 4$    **18.** $y = 1$    **19.** $x = 7$    **20.** $z = 6$    **21.** $k = 5$

**22.** $x = 9$    **23.** $z = 3$    **24.** $y = 1$    **25.** $y = 2$    **26.** $y = 7$    **27.** $k = 2$    **28.** $k = 7$

**29.** $k = 8$    **30.** $x = 2$    **31.** $z = 9$    **32.** $z = 9$    **33.** $x = 5$    **34.** $m = 8$    **35.** $x = 2$

**36.** $z = 7$    **37.** $k = 5$    **38.** $m = 2$

**Page 33:** Solving Equations

**1.** 52   **2.** 1   **3.** 93   **4.** 64   **5.** 1   **6.** 73   **7.** 12   **8.** 64   **9.** 4   **10.** 18

**Page 34:** Solving Equations

**1.** 14   **2.** 44   **3.** 2   **4.** 6   **5.** 11   **6.** 20   **7.** 5   **8.** 8   **9.** 12   **10.** 13

**Page 35:** Solving Equations

**1.** 1   **2.** 83   **3.** 16   **4.** -46   **5.** 77   **6.** 4   **7.** -15   **8.** 4   **9.** 77

**10.** 136

**Page 36:** Solving Equations

**1.** 11   **2.** 25   **3.** 23   **4.** -90   **5.** 59   **6.** 2   **7.** 31   **8.** 75   **9.** 47   **10.** 57

**Page 37:** Solving Equations

**1.** 11   **2.** 4   **3.** 1   **4.** -10   **5.** 5   **6.** 7   **7.** 23   **8.** 12   **9.** 11   **10.** 5

**Page 38:** Solving Equations

**1.** -2   **2.** 51   **3.** 11   **4.** 78   **5.** 36   **6.** 12   **7.** 13   **8.** 29   **9.** 0

**10.** -28

**Page 39:** Solving Equations

**1.** -34   **2.** 29   **3.** 10   **4.** 8   **5.** 55   **6.** 69   **7.** 96   **8.** 47   **9.** 111   **10.** 22

**Page 40:** Solving Equations

**1.** -3   **2.** 31   **3.** 51   **4.** 6   **5.** 8   **6.** 60   **7.** 3   **8.** 32   **9.** 6

**10.** -47

**Page 41:** Solving Equations

**1.** 49   **2.** 4   **3.** 5   **4.** 28   **5.** 10   **6.** 21   **7.** 5   **8.** 2   **9.** 1   **10.** 31

**Page 42:** Solving Inequalities

**1.** $x < 18$   **2.** $y \leq 6$   **3.** $z \leq 2$   **4.** $x > 8$   **5.** $k > 13$

**6.** k ≤ 0     **7.** y < -6/7     **8.** x < -12     **9.** x ≥ 9     **10.** m > 16

**11.** x ≤ 13     **12.** m ≥ 3/5     **13.** m ≤ 10     **14.** y > -1/3     **15.** k > 4

**16.** x < -42     **17.** x ≤ 6     **18.** z < -1     **19.** z > -13     **20.** x ≤ -1

**21.** y ≥ 7     **22.** z < -6     **23.** m ≤ -1     **24.** m ≤ 36     **25.** k > -18

**26.** k > 7     **27.** z ≤ 1     **28.** m ≥ -5/4

## Page 49: Simplify Expressions

**1.** 17y – 23     **2.** –20z + 1     **3.** –102m + 82     **4.** 3z + 8     **5.** 16y – 33

**6.** -31     **7.** 6y + 18     **8.** –10m     **9.** –16y – 14     **10.** –3z + 1

**11.** x – 12     **12.** –2k + 17     **13.** –9z + 15     **14.** 4m     **15.** –11z

**16.** –8m + 19     **17.** 20y + 12     **18.** 2y + 18     **19.** 3z – 25     **20.** –15y – 5

**21.** –19y     **22.** 18k + 26     **23.** 3m     **24.** 5x – 13

## Page 52: Graphing Linear Equations

**1.** $y = -3x + 1$

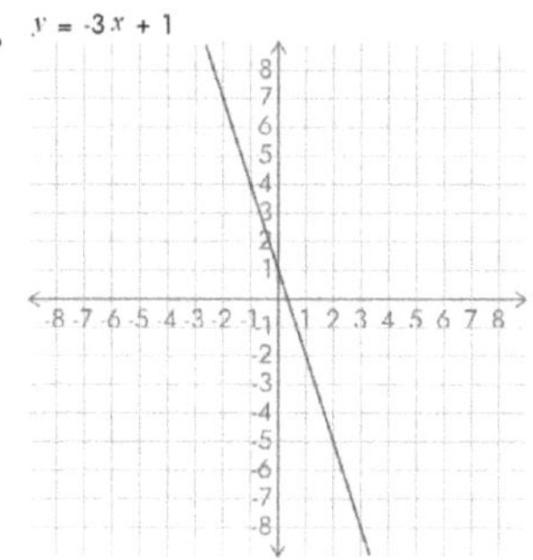

**2.** $y = \frac{1}{4}x + 5$

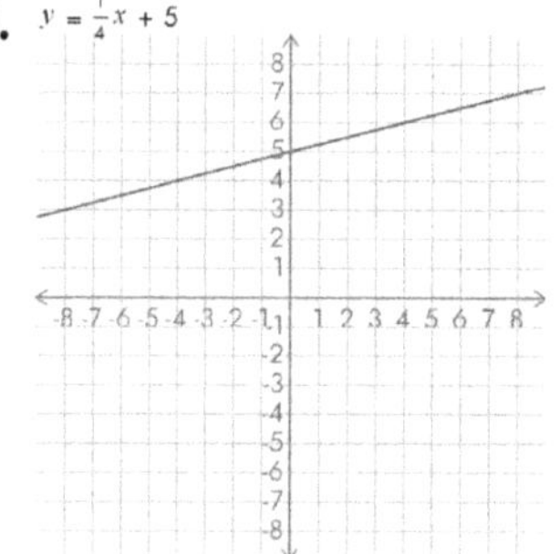

**3.** $y = \frac{5}{4}x - 4$

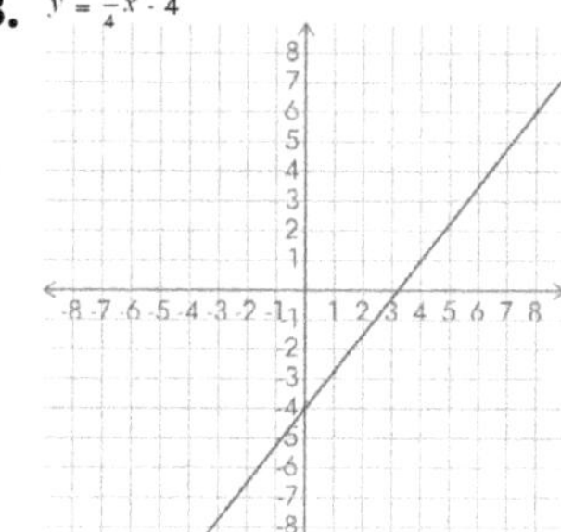

**4.** 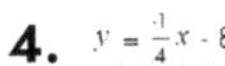  $y = \frac{-1}{4}x - 8$

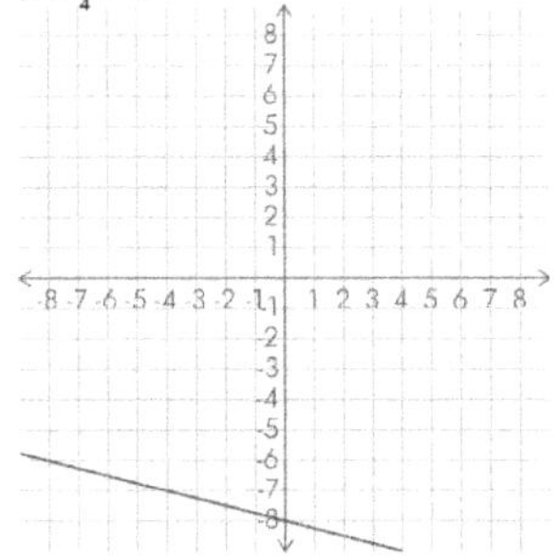

**5.** $y = \frac{3}{4}x - 6$

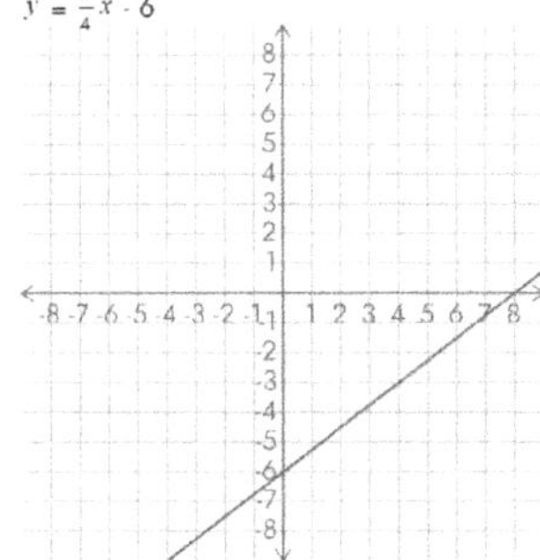